COOK ME A STORY

A treasury of stories and recipes inspired by classic fairy tales

BY BRYAN KOZLOWSKI

ILLUSTRATED BY LAURA WOOD

TABLE OF CONTENTS

BEFORE THE STORY BEGINS...

Watch out! Beware! You've entered into a kitchen tale.

No bedtime stories here. No hiding under the covers if the story gets scary. This is the land of kitchen tales, and that means adventure! You'll climb the beanstalk with Jack and get lost in the woods with Hansel and Gretel—but keep your eyes open! There are more monsters in the kitchen than in all fairyland, such as the hot stove that breathes fire like a dragon and knives as sharp as the Big Bad Wolf's teeth. Treat them carefully or they just might bite! If you stay on the recipe's path and follow the directions, you'll be safe. And whenever you need help, just do what Cinderella did—call on your fairy godmother (or father!).

A fairy wand will appear in the story whenever a grown-up helper is needed.
To start our kitchen adventure, we only need to say the deliciously magical words.
What were they again? Ah, yes…

ONCE UPON A KITCHEN...

4

STIRRINGS

TALES FOR BREAKFAST TIME

GOLDILOCKS AND THE THREE PEARS
Pear and Sweet Milk Porridge

❋

SLEEPING FRUITY
Sweet Kiss Strawberry Smoothie

❋

THREE LITTLE PIGS-IN-A-BUNDLE
Sausage and Hash Brown Stacks

❋

CINNARELLA
Cinnamon Pumpkin Pancakes

GOLDILOCKS & THE THREE PEARS

PEAR AND SWEET MILK PORRIDGE

Serves Two

THIS STORY NEEDS:

1 cup (250 ml) water
½ cup (50 g) quick-cooking oats
⅛ teaspoon salt
¼ cup (50 ml) sweetened condensed milk
1 cinnamon stick
3 large marshmallows
½ cup (145 g) chopped canned pears, drained

Once upon a time, there was a little round house with little round walls that stood in a corner of Stovey Woods. Every morning the family of pears who lived inside the little round house made a pot of porridge for their breakfast.

 Place a small pot on the stove. Put the water, oats, and salt into the pot and stir them together.

After they hung the pot over the fire, they went out for a walk in the woods while their porridge cooked.

 Turn on the stove to medium heat.

While they were out, a little girl named Goldilocks came to the house. She looked very sweet, but she was also very naughty. She had smelled the porridge cooking and wanted a taste.

 Add the sweetened condensed milk to the pot.

PAPA PEAR

BABY PEAR

MAMA PEAR

7

After she tasted the porridge, she decided to sit down and rest. But Goldilocks was too big for the little chair—she broke off one of its wooden legs!

 Add the cinnamon stick to the pot.

Goldilocks then went upstairs and tested out the three beds. The first was too hard, and the second was too soft, but the last one was just right. There she fell fast asleep.

 Add the three marshmallows to the pot.

The pear family heard their porridge bubbling, and came back home from their morning walk. "Somebody has been eating our porridge and sitting in our chairs!" said the pears. When they found Goldilocks laying in one of their beds, they chased her all around the house.

When the porridge starts to bubble, add the chopped pears to the pot. Stir the porridge and cook until the marshmallows have fully melted.

Goldilocks was so scared that she tripped over the broken chair and tumbled out of the house. Then the pears sat down to their breakfast and ate happily ever after, never seeing Goldilocks again.

Take the pot off the heat and, with your spoon, remove the cinnamon stick from the porridge. Spoon into bowls and eat it up before Goldilocks takes a bite of yours!

SLEEPING FRUITY

SWEET KISS STRAWBERRY SMOOTHIE

Serves Two

THIS STORY NEEDS:

8 ounces (230 g) fresh strawberries, stems removed
3 tablespoons sugar
½ cup (125 ml) half-and-half (single cream)
1 kiwi, peeled
¼ teaspoon vanilla extract
1 banana, peeled
Ice cubes

In a kingdom far away, there was a tall glass castle where a beautiful baby princess was born. Her skin was as red as a rose and she looked just as sweet as a berry.

 Put the strawberries into a blender.

On her first birthday, three good fairies came to the castle to give the princess their magical wishes. From the first fairy's wand came a shower of crystal sparkles, and she said, "Nature's treat, I'll complete, may you be forever sweet."

 Add the sugar to the blender.

From the second fairy's wand came a stream of pure white, and she said, "Glistening cream, see it gleam, may you live a happy dream."

 Pour the half-and-half (cream) into the blender.

Then out of nowhere, a wicked fairy appeared. Angry at not being invited, she pointed her wand at the princess and said, "I have my own fruity for this little beauty. It's sour and green, and here's something mean: the princess will die when she turns fifteen!"

 *Add the kiwi to the blender.*

Everyone was horrified, but the last good fairy still had one magical gift left. Out of her wand came the loveliest-smelling wish of them all. And she said, "I'll turn that curse into a sleep of bliss, until she wakes by a loving kiss."

 Add the vanilla extract to the blender.

As the child grew, the king and queen did everything to protect her from harm. But they forgot about a pointy yellow spindle hidden away in the highest tower of the castle.

Add the banana to the blender.

And, just like the wicked fairy had said, when the princess turned fifteen, she went up into the highest tower, pricked her finger on the spindle, and fell into a frozen sleep. While she slept, the princess snored so loudly that she shook and rumbled the entire castle.

Add a handful of ice cubes to the blender (about 8). With the lid in place, turn on the blender until the mixture is smooth and the ice is crushed.

After many years, a traveling prince heard the loud rumble and found the princess sleeping inside the castle. She looked beautiful and sweet, so he kissed her. And just as he did, Sleeping Fruity awoke, her long sleep finally over.

Pour the smoothie into glasses, add a straw, and have a "kiss" for yourself.

13

THREE LITTLE PIGS-IN-A-BUNDLE

SAUSAGE AND HASH BROWN STACKS

Serves Three

THIS STORY NEEDS:

3 fully cooked sausages
3 cups (220 g) frozen shredded hash browns
1 scallion (spring onion), sliced
½ red bell pepper, chopped
1 egg, beaten
¼ teaspoon salt

Preheat oven to 400°F
(200°C)

O nce upon a time, on a warm summer's day, three little pigs trotted into an empty field and decided to build themselves three little houses.

Place the sausages on a non-stick (or parchment-lined) baking tray and set them aside.

The first pig, being very lazy, went over to a nearby haystack and said, "I'll use this straw to make my nest, and then I'll have more time to rest!"

Put the hash browns into a large mixing bowl.

The second pig, being very silly, pulled up a sprig of grass in the field and said, "A house of grass is built quicker than hay, and then I'll have more time to play!"

 Add the sliced scallions (spring onions) to the mixing bowl.

But the third pig, being very smart, bought some red bricks and yellow glue and said, "Straw is weak and grass is quick, but I'll be safe in my house of brick!" The smart pig was right—a hungry wolf was waiting (with some salt) to eat the little pigs for his breakfast. With one enormous breath, he huffed and he puffed and he smashed down the two flimsy houses of straw and grass.

Add the chopped bell pepper and the beaten egg to the mixing bowl. Add the salt and smash everything together with a spoon until combined.

Squealing in fright, the lazy pig and the silly pig picked up what was left of their little homes and ran inside their brother's sturdy house of brick. The wolf thought he could just as easily blow down the smart pig's house, but the bricks and glue that held it together were getting harder and stronger in the hot summer sun.

Using your hands, mound the hash brown mixture equally over each sausage on the baking tray, and then put it into the oven.

With all his might, the wolf huffed and puffed, and puffed and huffed, but the bricks wouldn't budge. The three little pigs stayed safe and toasty inside their little home. All huffed out without a puff of air left in him, the wolf gave up and waddled off without one pig for his breakfast. But maybe *you* can make something for him...

Bake the sausage stacks for 30 minutes. Using oven mitts, remove the tray from the oven and transfer the sausage stacks to a plate with a spatula. Give them your best huff and puff and see if you can get inside.

CINNARELLA

CINNAMON PUMPKIN PANCAKES

Serves Two

THIS STORY NEEDS:

2 teaspoons ground cinnamon
½ cup (70 g) flour
¾ teaspoon baking powder
2 tablespoons dark brown sugar
2 tablespoons canned pumpkin
⅔ cup (150 ml) half-and-half (single cream)
1½ tablespoons (21 g) butter

Long ago, there was a poor girl named Cinnarella who lived in a bowl-shaped house with her ugly stepsisters. The selfish stepsisters made Cinnarella cook for them and clean the entire house, so Cinnarella was always covered in white, powdery dust from her head to her feet.

 Put the cinnamon into a large mixing bowl.
Add the flour and baking powder.

One day, an invitation to a royal ball arrived from the palace. Because the stepsisters kept Cinnarella busy sewing their ugly brown dresses, she had no time to make a dress for herself.

 Add the brown sugar to the bowl
and stir everything together.

Left all alone without any chance of going to the ball, Cinnarella began to cry. Suddenly she noticed a pumpkin outside in the garden that was growing bigger and bigger, as if by magic.

 Add the canned pumpkin to the bowl.

It was the magic of her fairy godmother! After her godmother turned the pumpkin into a carriage, she made a beautiful dress and shoes for Cinnarella. The fairy godmother twirled her wand around Cinnarella once more and said, "Now you are the prettiest girl of all. Whisk away, whisk away, off to the ball!"

Pour the half-and-half (cream) into the bowl. Whisk until the batter is smooth, without any large lumps. Set the bowl aside.

At the palace, the ballroom floor was shiny and polished for the dancers. When Cinnarella arrived at the palace, a handsome prince welcomed her, led her to the ballroom floor, and asked her to dance.

 Put a griddle (or large non-stick skillet) on top of the stove, add the butter, and turn the heat to medium. When the butter begins to bubble, pour the pancake batter onto the griddle in four small rounds.

Cinnarella was whirled and flipped about so much while dancing that she lost her shoe. She quickly ran out of the palace, afraid the prince would see her dusty foot.

 When small bubbles appear in the center of the pancakes, flip each one over with a spatula and cook for one more minute. Then remove the pancakes to a plate.

Trying to find Cinnarella again, the prince hosted another ball, dancing and flipping the remaining ladies of the kingdom to discover if any of them were missing a shoe.

 Turn the heat down to low and cook the remaining batter as before.

At long last, the prince found Cinnarella—who was indeed missing a shoe! He didn't care if she was poor or had dusty feet. He loved her just as plain as she was. Well, perhaps a bath of golden syrup wouldn't hurt.

 Remove the second batch of pancakes to the plate and drizzle with syrup, if you'd like.

SNACKINGS
TALES FOR ANYTIME

JACK AND THE GREEN BEANSTALK
Crispy Beanstalk Fries

❀

RAPRETZEL
Braided Pretzel Twists

❀

BEAUTY AND THE BROCKLY BEAST
Bacon Dip for Beastly Broccoli

JACK AND THE GREEN BEANSTALK

CRISPY BEANSTALK FRIES

Serves Four

THIS STORY NEEDS:

1 large plastic resealable bag
6 ounces (170 g) fresh green beans, stems removed
1 tablespoon milk
2 tablespoons flour
2 tablespoons vegetable oil
½ cup (45 g) seasoned panko-style breadcrumbs
Salt

Preheat oven to 425°F (220°C)

There once was a very poor and very hungry boy named Jack. One day an old man took pity on him and gave him a bag of magic beans saying, "Bury these deep in your garden and you'll never be hungry again." Jack did just as the old man said and then went straight to bed. That night, little white raindrops fell from the sky, landing right on top of the mound of buried beans.

Open the bag and put the green beans inside. Pour the milk into the bag, seal it closed, and shake until the beans are coated with milk.

In the middle of Jack's garden, a giant beanstalk had sprouted up to the sky. So Jack did what all adventurous boys would do; he climbed it. He went up and up and up, straight through the white, powdery clouds above.

Put the flour in the bag, seal it closed, and shake until the beans are coated with flour.

At the very top of the beanstalk, there was a giant castle with a giant door and a giant-sized woman carrying a giant bottle of cooking oil.

 Pour the oil into the bag, seal it closed, and shake until the beans are coated with oil.

"This is no place for a boy!" shouted the woman. "My husband will eat you for a snack!" But Jack had no time to escape, for at that very moment, her husband entered the kitchen. Quickly, the woman told Jack to hide in a giant bowl of breadcrumbs.

Put the breadcrumbs in the bag, seal it closed, and shake well until the beans are coated with breadcrumbs.

"Fee-fi-fo-foy, I smell the blood of an English boy," said the giant.

"Yes!" said his wife. "I'm cooking you a baked boy! Now take a little nap and it will be done when you wake." The woman rushed outside, snapped off pieces of the beanstalk, and put them on a tray. The beanstalks then went into the oven (instead of Jack) and the giant went to sleep, not realizing that his wife had tricked him or that Jack was now safely climbing back down the beanstalk.

Open the bag and carefully arrange the green beans on a non-stick baking tray so that they are not touching one another. Put the tray into the oven and cook for 12 to 16 minutes, or until the green beans are golden brown.

The giant awoke and saw what was really cooking in the oven. In a fit of rage, he threw the tray of beanstalks out into the clouds, and down they fell onto Jack's house—crispy, delicious, and ready to eat. Jack gathered them all up and was never hungry again.

Using oven mitts, remove the tray from the oven and sprinkle the green beans with a pinch of salt.

RAPRETZEL

BRAIDED PRETZEL TWISTS

Makes Ten

THIS STORY NEEDS:

1 cup (250 ml) warm water
2 tablespoons baking soda (bicarbonate of soda)
1 can (11 ounces / 311 g) refrigerated
French bread (or pizza) dough
¼ teaspoon kosher salt
2 tablespoons (28 g) butter, melted

Preheat oven to 375°F (190°C)

In a distant land, a woman was walking through the forest with her child when she came upon a small well. The well belonged to an evil witch, but the woman was thirsty and the water looked refreshing. So she took a sip.

Put the warm water and baking soda into a large bowl. Stir until the baking soda is dissolved and set the bowl aside.

"Thief!" cried the witch in anger. "You stole my water, so I'll steal your child!" Before the woman knew what had happened, her little child, who felt like a doughy bundle in her arms, was snatched away by the evil witch. The witch took the child to a high tower in the middle of the forest. There Rapretzel grew, and so did her hair. Indeed, her hair grew so fast it had to be cut nine times!

Open the can of dough and place it on a cutting board. Make sure the log of dough is about 10 inches (25 cm) long. Cut the log of dough nine times to make ten thin round slices, each about an inch wide.

Eventually, the witch stopped cutting Rapretzel's hair and instead decided to use her long hair as a rope to climb up and down from the high tower.

Using your hands, roll each round of dough into thin ropes, about 12 inches (30 cm) long.

Day after day, Rapretzel sat lonely in the tower, braiding her long hair and letting it hang out the window. One day, a handsome prince noticed the strange rope of hair dangling from the tower. He climbed it and reached the top. When Rapretzel and the prince saw one another, they both fell instantly in love. But the witch hated love more than anything else, and when she saw them together, she threw them out of the tower and into the watery well below.

One rope of dough at a time, fold the two ends over each other until they form a braided twist. Dip each pretzel into the baking-soda water and place them on a non-stick baking tray.

At this, Rapretzel cried salty tears, but the witch wasn't finished with her yet. She cursed her and the prince to a hot wilderness and said, "Let's see if love will save you there!"

 Sprinkle each pretzel with a little kosher salt, and put the tray into the oven.

In the hot wilderness, Rapretzel and her prince remained locked in each other's arms. They didn't die because the witch was wrong. Love is magic, and it saved them. Rapretzel's beautiful hair grew more golden than ever in the hot wilderness. It glistened like sweet summer butter. In fact, it really looked good enough to eat.

 Cook the pretzels for 10 to 12 minutes, or until golden brown. Using oven mitts, remove the tray from the oven and, with a basting brush, coat the tops of the pretzels with the melted butter. Then go on, take a bite. Rapretzel won't mind.

BEAUTY AND THE BROCKLY BEAST

BACON DIP FOR BEASTLY BROCCOLI

Serves Six

THIS STORY NEEDS:

1 head of broccoli
1 packet (2.8 ounces / 79 g) real bacon pieces
8 ounces (227 g) sour cream
8 ounces (227 g) cream cheese, cut into small chunks
1 cup (113 g) shredded cheddar cheese
2 tablespoons chopped fresh chives
2 teaspoons ranch seasoning mix (or ranch dressing)

In a distant kingdom, there lived a hideous beast deep inside a dark castle. He had green skin and an enormous hairy head, but no one knew for sure because no one dared go near the castle to find out.

Snap off the broccoli florets from the top of the stalks and set the florets aside.

One day, a curious pig farmer set out on a journey, with a bag full of bacon, to see if he could lure the beast with the smell of the delicious meat. Once the farmer arrived at the castle, the monster leapt upon him and growled, "I am the Brockly Beast! How dare you enter my house?" The Beast then locked him in the dungeon and threw him a measly bowl of soured cream for his supper.

Put the bacon pieces into a large microwave-safe bowl. Add the sour cream.

The farmer's beautiful and brave daughter—who had creamy-white skin—traveled to the castle alone to make a deal with the Beast and rescue her father. She promised to stay with the Beast forever if he agreed to let her father go free. The Beast accepted the offer and soon began to love the farmer's daughter, whom he called Beauty. Every day, the Beast gave Beauty gifts of yellow gold in order to make her love him in return. But Beauty only feared the monster.

Add the cream cheese and the cheddar cheese to the bowl.

Thinking that no one could love an ugly beast like himself, he walked outside and fell lifeless upon the green grass, as if he had died of a broken heart. Just then, a fairy appeared and knelt beside the Beast saying, "Because you've loved Beauty without strife, you shall have a human life." She sprinkled magic dust upon him.

 *Add the chives and the ranch mix
(or dressing) to the bowl.*

Her magic was powerful; the Beast began to spin around and around. From her wand came flashes of bright light and a warm wind that whirled like a hurricane.

 *Stir all the ingredients together and put the bowl into the
microwave, heating for 1 to 2 minutes, until the cheese
is melted and the dip is warm.*

Beauty watched this magic in amazement and rushed to the Beast's side, no longer afraid of the monster. But he was a monster no longer! The fairy had turned him into a handsome prince. And they loved and lived happily together, forever.

Carefully remove the bowl from the microwave, stir the dip once more, and serve with the now not-so-beastly broccoli.

SUPPINGS
TALES FOR LUNCH & DINNER TIME

LITTLE RED ROMA HOOD
Picnic-Basket Stuffed Tomatoes

❀

THE PRINCESS AND THE PEA PATTIES
Green Pea "Mini-Mattress" Burgers

❀

THREE CHILI GOATS PUFF
Chili-Puff Troll Rolls

❀

RUMPASTALSKIN
Golden Straws Spaghetti Pie

LITTLE RED ROMA HOOD

PICNIC-BASKET STUFFED TOMATOES

Makes Six

THIS STORY NEEDS:

6 Roma (or plum) tomatoes
¼ cup (20 g) seasoned panko-style breadcrumbs
¼ cup (28 g) shredded cheddar cheese
¼ cup (60 g) condensed cream of mushroom soup
1 scallion (spring onion), thinly sliced
Ground black pepper

Preheat oven to 400°F (200°C)

In a far away land, there was a little girl who received a lovely present from her grandmother: a pretty hood made of the reddest cloth—as red as a Roma tomato. She loved it and wore it so often that she came to be called Little Red Roma Hood.

Cut a thin slice from the stem end of each tomato so they stand upright. Cut the tops off, and scoop out the insides with a small measuring spoon. Set the tomatoes and their tops aside.

To thank her grandmother for the gift, Little Red Roma Hood packed a picnic basket with bread and cheese and set off towards her grandmother's house deep within the woods. Along the way, Little Red Roma Hood met a wolf who was standing atop a mound of woodland mushrooms. The wolf slyly asked, "Where are you going this fine afternoon?"

Put the breadcrumbs and shredded cheese into a large mixing bowl. Add the mushroom soup.

Little Red Roma Hood told him about the picnic she was bringing to her grandmother, and the wolf replied, "Mmm…sounds delicious, but wouldn't Grandmother like some scallions too? There's a nice bunch of them growing wild in the woods." So while Little Red Roma Hood stopped to pick scallions, the wolf ran straight to Grandmother's house, sprinkled some pepper on the old lady, and gobbled her right up.

 Add the sliced scallions (spring onions) to the bowl. Add a pinch of black pepper and stir everything together.

When Little Red Roma Hood finally arrived at Grandmother's house, she knew something was wrong. The wolf was in Grandmother's bed! But before she had time to escape, the wolf took one big bite (without chewing!) and stuffed her into his belly, picnic basket and all.

Stuff each tomato with the breadcrumb mixture, and then top each tomato with its top.

After such a big meal, the wolf fell into a deep sleep. Meanwhile, Little Red Roma Hood and Grandmother waited in his dark belly, certain they would never see the light of day again.

Put the tomatoes on a non-stick baking tray and cook them in the oven for 25 minutes.

But luckily a huntsman was passing by and heard the wolf snoring. He rushed inside the house and leapt upon the wolf's belly. Out popped Little Red Roma Hood, Grandmother, and the picnic basket, all ready for lunch. The wolf, however, slouched off with a terrible bellyache.

Using oven mitts, remove the tray from the oven and let the tomatoes cool slightly before eating.

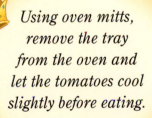

THE PRINCESS AND THE PEA PATTIES

GREEN PEA "MINI-MATTRESS" BURGERS

Serves Two

THIS STORY NEEDS:

1 cup (140 g) frozen peas
¼ cup (55 g) mayonnaise
4 teaspoons dry onion soup mix
½ cup (30 g) plain instant mashed potato flakes
2 tablespoons flour
1 tablespoon butter

In a kingdom far away, there was a terrible storm that rained down upon the land. Every cloud burst open and soaked the green earth in great big puddles.

 Put the frozen peas into a large mixing bowl, and fill the bowl with hot water. Let the peas soak for 5 minutes.

In the middle of the storm, there was a knock on the castle door. The prince went to open it and saw a princess standing outside in the rain, dripping wet. The prince invited the princess inside and ordered his servants to dry her off. They began squeezing, squashing, and mashing the wetness from her.

 Drain the peas into a colander and return them to the dry mixing bowl. Using your hands (or the bottom of a plastic cup), mash the peas until all are split open.

The servants dressed the princess in a white fluffy nightgown and gave her a bowl of onion soup for supper.

Add the mayonnaise and onion soup mix to the mixing bowl and stir. Then add the potato flakes and the flour and stir until well combined.

The prince gathered all the mattresses in the castle and placed a little green pea at the bottom of the pile saying, "If our visitor can feel this pea under all of these soft mattresses, then that means she's a real princess and I'll make her my wife."

Shape the mixture into four small, round patties and set them aside on a plate.

After her supper, the princess was led to the tower of mattresses. But climbing to the top was no easy task! The mattresses were so soft that they were almost slippery. It was like climbing up a stick of melting butter.

Put the butter into a large, non-stick skillet and place it on the stove over medium heat.

That night, the princess hardly slept a wink. She was constantly tossing and flipping about on the mattresses and could not get comfortable.

When the butter begins to bubble, place the patties into the skillet. Cook on one side until browned (3 to 4 minutes), and then flip the patties over with a spatula and cook for another 2 to 3 minutes.

In the morning, the prince asked the princess how she had slept. "Oh just terrible!" said the princess. "There was something very hard under all those mattresses!" And she was right! Anyone who can detect a little pea under a lot of pillows must be a true princess indeed!

With the spatula, transfer the burgers to a plate and see if you can find the little peas as well.

THREE CHILI GOATS PUFF

CHILI-PUFF TROLL ROLLS

Makes Eight

THIS STORY NEEDS:

Non-stick cooking spray
1 can (16.3 ounces / 462 g) refrigerated croissant rolls
1 can (10 ounces / 283 g) chili with meat
½ cup (56 g) shredded cheddar cheese

Preheat oven to 350°F (180°C)

Far away, over hills of pots and peaks of pans, was a beautiful place called Muffin-Tin Meadow where the grass always sparkled in the glistening sun. Everyone wanted to go to Muffin-Tin Meadow, but no one could cross the bridge because a big, hungry troll lived under it. He liked to squash and smash and eat up anyone who tried.

In a 12-cup muffin tin, spray 8 empty spaces with non-stick cooking spray and set the tin aside. Open the can of croissants and, one at a time, smash and press each roll into a 5-inch flat round.

But one day, three chili goats decided that the grass in Muffin-Tin Meadow looked too good to resist. They stirred up their courage and made their way to the bridge.

Pour the chili into a small bowl and give it a quick stir.

The first goat got halfway across the bridge when he saw the troll. The first goat said, "You don't want to eat me. Wait for my bigger brother. There's much more chili to squeeze out of him." So the troll let the first goat pass.

 Put one level tablespoon of chili onto the middle of each flattened croissant.

The second goat hardly stepped onto the bridge before the troll tried to bite him. The second goat said, "You don't want to bite me. Wait for my biggest brother. He's the one that tastes like cheese." So the troll let the second goat pass.

 Sprinkle the cheddar cheese evenly onto each mound of chili.

Now the third goat was indeed the biggest—even bigger than the troll! To teach the monster a lesson, he leapt onto the bridge, smashed into the troll, pinched him all over, and threw him into the river below.

One at a time, pull the sides of the croissant up over the cheese and chili and pinch the ends together to form a tight seal on top. Place each croissant, seal-side down, into the muffin tin.

At last, all was safe and the three chili goats trotted together into Muffin-Tin Meadow where the grass always sparkled in the glistening sun.

 Put the muffin tin into the oven and cook for 17 minutes, or until the tops of the rolls are golden brown.

The chili goats ate so much grass in the meadow that even the smaller two grew big and puffy—big enough to make sure that no troll ever lived under the bridge again.

 Using oven mitts, remove the muffin tin from the oven. Let the rolls cool for 10 minutes before eating.

RUMPASTALSKIN

GOLDEN STRAWS SPAGHETTI PIE

Serves Two

THIS STORY NEEDS:

8 ounces (227 g) thin spaghetti
1 tablespoon yellow mustard
1¼ cups (300 ml) water
⅛ teaspoon salt
1 jar (15 ounces / 425 g) Alfredo sauce
¼ teaspoon ground turmeric

Preheat oven to 400°F (200°C)

In a small village, there lived a miller who had a beautiful daughter. One day he received a visit from the king. To make himself look important, the miller claimed his daughter could spin straw into gold.

 Put the uncooked spaghetti into a large bowl.

The king was a greedy man. He ordered the miller's daughter to the palace the following day, putting her into a room full of broken bits of straw.

Grabbing a small handful of spaghetti at a time, break each of the long strands in half, then break each half in half again. Lay the broken spaghetti crisscrossed in a 9-inch (23 cm) pie pan.

Before locking her in the room, the king tossed her a pot of yellow mustard and said, "If you can't make all the straw as yellow as this mustard, then your father has lied to me and tomorrow you shall die." The miller's daughter was hopelessly lost. She didn't know the first thing about turning straw into gold, so she sat there and cried big puddles of salty tears.

 Put the mustard into a separate mixing bowl. Then add the water and salt.

Suddenly, an ugly goblin appeared and said, "Here I am, all be told, to turn this straw into gold!" He pulled out two jars of magical ingredients: one white and one yellow. He mixed them both together and danced around the room, sprinkling the magical mixture over all the broken bits of straw. He sang loudly, "Look at me! Such a fellow! Soon this all will be yellow!"

 Add the Alfredo sauce and turmeric to the water and stir everything together. Pour the Alfredo mixture over the broken spaghetti in the pie pan.

The miller's daughter thought she had been saved, until the goblin turned to her and said, "Silly lady, this ain't for you! Remember, goblins like gold too! We smash it into a scrumptious pie and eat it up, eat it up, eat it up dry!" But goblins love games even more than they love gold, so he gave the miller's daughter one hour to guess his name before the straw turned yellow. If she guessed correctly, he wouldn't eat a bit of it.

Make sure all the spaghetti pieces are submerged in the sauce. Tightly seal the top of the pie pan with aluminum foil and place it in the oven for one hour.

After going through every name she knew, the miller's daughter was just about to give up when the goblin made one mistake. Thinking he had already won, he took a nap and started singing in his sleep: "She'll never guess! I've won this game! 'Cause Rumpastalskin is my name!" When the goblin woke up and realized his mistake, he disappeared in an angry cloud of steam. The straw had turned to gold, and the Miller's daughter was saved! She never needed Rumpastalskin again.

Using oven mitts, remove the pie from the oven, but keep it covered for an additional 10 minutes. No peeking! Uncover the pie pan and see if goblin gold is as delicious as Rumpastalskin said.

SWEETINGS
TALES FOR DESSERT TIME

HANSEL AND GREGGTEL
"A House Made of Cake" Cookies

❀

PLUMBELINA
Sugar Plum Fairy Cakes

❀

SNOW WHITE AND THE SEVEN DUMPLINGS
Sticky Apple Dumplings

HANSEL AND GREGGTEL

"A HOUSE MADE OF CAKE" COOKIES

Makes 12 to 14 cookies

THIS STORY NEEDS:

2 eggs

5 tablespoons (70 g) butter, softened

1 box (15.25 ounces / 432 g) yellow cake mix

¼ teaspoon ground cinnamon

1 teaspoon sugar

Parchment paper

Non-stick cooking spray

Preheat oven to 350°F (180°C)

t the edge of a great forest, a poor woodcutter and his wife lived with their two children. The boy and girl were always as bright and sunny as the inside of an egg, and so they were called Hansel and Greggtel. The family never had enough to eat, and the wife always blamed the children. "Those little brats have eaten all the bread and butter in the house," she told her husband, "and either they leave or we all starve to death!"

 Crack the eggs into a large mixing bowl. Add the softened butter.

The wife led the children deep into the forest. She led them around in circles to get them lost, and then she left them all alone.

With a whisk, stir the eggs and butter around in the bowl until combined.

As hard as they tried, Hansel and Greggtel couldn't find their way back home. Suddenly, they came upon a house in the middle of the forest made entirely of cake! Desperately hungry, the children ran towards the house, plunged their hands into the walls and windows, and started eating up the scrumptious little home.

Add the cake mix to the mixing bowl. Using clean hands, mix (and squish!) all the ingredients until fully combined.

Just then, the door opened wide and out sprang a very ugly old woman. She snatched Hansel and Greggtel and threw them into the cold cellar beneath her house. She was a wicked witch who loved to trap, cook, and eat lost little children.

Put the mixing bowl into the freezer for 20 minutes.

While the children were shivering in the cold cellar, the witch prepared her kitchen to cook them. She turned on her oven, got out her pans, and made a special seasoning of sugar and spice.

Line a cookie sheet with parchment paper and combine the sugar and cinnamon in a separate small bowl.

Once all was ready, the witch grabbed the children and, with her greasy hands, squashed them onto the pan and sprinkled them with sugar and spice.

Remove the mixing bowl from the freezer and coat your hands with non-stick spray. Make 12 to 14 little balls out of the dough, and place them onto the parchment-lined cookie sheet. Flatten each dough ball and sprinkle with the cinnamon sugar.

But Hansel and Greggtel were much more clever than the witch. When she got them close to the oven, they pushed her inside instead. In the oven, the witch turned into what all witches become when baked. They might not be pretty and they might not be nice, but when witches are cooked, they turn into sugar and spice.

Put the cookie sheet in the oven for 10 minutes. Using oven mitts, remove the cookies from the oven and let them cool on the sheet for 10 minutes before eating.

PLUMBELINA

SUGAR PLUM FAIRY CAKES

Makes 12 mini cakes

THIS STORY NEEDS:

12 paper baking cups
2 plums, pitted and chopped small
6 teaspoons sugar
½ cup (70 g) flour
1¼ teaspoons baking powder
1 can (14 ounces / 396 g) sweetened condensed milk
1 egg, beaten
5 tablespoons (70 g) butter, melted

Preheat oven to 350°F (180°C)

Long ago, there was an old woman who wished for a child of her own. A kind fairy took pity on her and gave the woman a special flower with papery petals. "A flower to make your wish come true," said the fairy.

Line a 12-cup muffin tin with the paper baking cups. Spray the inside of each cup with non-stick cooking spray.

It was a special flower indeed! For as soon as the old woman took it home, the petals opened up and inside sat a very tiny girl. She was no bigger than a plum, so the old woman called her Plumbelina. Since Plumbelina was so tiny and delicate, the old woman gave her a spoonful of sugar every day to make her grow. But no matter how much sugar she ate, Plumbelina never grew.

Place a small amount of chopped plums inside each paper cup. Sprinkle ½ teaspoon of sugar over the plums in each cup and set the muffin tin aside.

One day a little white mouse made friends with Plumbelina. "I know why you're not growing!" said the mouse. "You must be a mouse! Come and live with me in my little hole where it's nice and dry and there's lots of soft dust to sit upon."

 In a mixing bowl, stir the flour and baking powder together and set it aside.

"No, no, she's not a mouse!" said another voice. A toad hopped up onto the windowsill. "She is a toad! Come and live with me in the pond where it's nice and wet and there's lots of slime to sit upon."

 In a separate large bowl, stir the condensed milk, the beaten egg, and melted butter until combined.

Plumbelina first tried living with the mouse, but it was too dusty. Then she tried living with the toad, but it was too slimy. She didn't seem to fit in anywhere at all.

Add the flour mixture to the milk mixture and stir them together until combined. It's okay if the batter is lumpy.

Covered in dust and slime, Plumbelina crawled back inside her flower and cried. "If I'm not a mouse and I'm not a toad, then what am I?" Just then, Plumbelina felt a gentle kiss on her cheek. It came from a fairy prince. He dried her tears, took her hand, and led her out of the window into the warm, golden sunshine.

Pour two tablespoons of the batter over the plums in each cup. Be sure not to fill the cups more than halfway full. Put the muffin tin into the oven for 20 minutes, or until the tops of the cakes are golden brown.

"You're a fairy, Plumbelina, can't you see?" said the prince. She turned around to see what he meant. The warm sun on her skin had made Plumbelina sprout wings. She was a fairy, after all! And off she flew with the prince to her new home in the sky.

Using oven mitts, remove the cakes from the oven and let them cool for 10 minutes. Then carefully peel off their paper cups and turn each one upside down.

SNOW WHITE AND THE SEVEN DUMPLINGS

STICKY APPLE DUMPLINGS

Makes Eight

THIS STORY NEEDS:

1 Gala apple
1 can (8 ounces / 226 g) refrigerated croissant rolls
4 tablespoons (56 g) salted butter
¼ cup (55 g) sugar
1 cup (250 ml) apple juice

Preheat oven to 350° F (180° C)

In a far off castle, a child with rosy red cheeks and skin as white as snow was born and named Snow White. Everyone in the castle loved her, except for the evil queen, who hated anyone who was more beautiful than she. Full of envy, the queen vowed to have Snow White killed. But the child overheard her plans and escaped into the dark forest. Running as fast as she could, she stumbled over sharp rocks and thorns that cut through her snow-white skin.

Peel the apple with a vegetable peeler. Cut the apple into eight wedges. Cut the seeds away from each wedge to remove the hard core. Set the apple wedges aside.

When daylight brightened the forest, Snow White saw a little cottage in the distance with pleasant little men working outside. Each dwarf wore a soft, triangle-shaped hat on top of his little head. Full of tears, Snow White told the dwarfs how the queen had tried to kill her. "There, there, child, you can stay here with us," said the dwarfs. They gave her a little triangle hat of her own, wrapped her in soft blankets, and kept her safe inside their cottage.

Open the can of croissant rolls, carefully unroll the dough, and separate each triangle. Place one apple wedge on each triangle and roll the dough around the apple. Place them in a 9-by-13-inch (23-by-33-cm) baking dish and set aside.

Meanwhile, the evil queen couldn't rest until Snow White was dead and gone. So she descended into the deepest dungeon of the castle and brewed a poisonous potion, sweet and sticky.

Put the butter and sugar into a small pot and place it on the stove over medium heat. Stir until the butter is melted, then remove from the heat and set it aside.

The queen disguised herself as an old woman with a basket full of apples and traveled to the home of the seven dwarfs where Snow White was all alone. "Apples bright, come take a bite," sang the queen, "So juicy, so sweet, so lovely a treat." Snow White held out her hand for one, unaware they were coated in the queen's sticky sweet poison. As soon as Snow White took a bite, she fell to the ground, asleep.

Pour the apple juice around the dumplings in the baking dish. Spoon the melted butter and sugar evenly over the tops of each dumpling.

When the dwarfs returned home, they saw Snow White lying on the ground. They wept for the beautiful girl and put her tenderly into a warm glass coffin because they couldn't bring themselves to bury her in the cold, dark earth.

Put the baking dish in the oven for 30 minutes.

One day, a prince passed through the forest. Overcome with love at the sight of Snow White, he bent down and touched her cheek with a tender kiss. And since kisses cure every evil, Snow White opened her eyes and lived again, happily ever after.

Using oven mitts, remove the baking dish from the oven. Scoop out the dumplings with a spatula and serve with the queen's sticky sweet syrup in the dish…if you dare!

SIPPINGS
TALES FOR THIRSTY TIME

THE LITTLE MERM-ADE
Sea Foam Blue Lemonade

❀

THE FIZZY FROG PRINCE
Sparkling Green-Slime Punch

❀

THE UGLY CHOCLING
White Swans Hot Chocolate

THE LITTLE MERM-ADE

SEA FOAM BLUE LEMONADE

Makes Nine Cups

THIS STORY NEEDS:

4 cups (1 L) cold water
¾ cup (175 g) frozen lemonade concentrate
Blue food dye
Pineapple sherbet or sorbet (about 1 cup / 250 ml)
4 cups (1 L) lemon lime soda

Far out at sea, where the water is as clear as glass, there lived a little mermaid who loved to watch humans as they sailed their mighty ships across the calm waves. One day, a great, icy storm descended upon the ocean and stirred up the restless waves. The waves tossed the ships up and down until a giant gush of water swept one sailor overboard.

Pour the water into a large glass bowl or large pitcher.
Add the lemonade concentrate to the bowl and stir until dissolved.

Swimming to the sailor, the mermaid clutched him in her arms and swam him to safety. He was very near death, so the mermaid shed one magical blue tear over him. The sailor immediately woke up, wondering who had saved him.

Add one drop of blue food coloring to the bowl, but do not stir.

71

But the mermaid had already plunged back into the ocean and was swimming down to the deep blue cave where the old Sea Witch lived. The sailor had awoken the mermaid's desire to be human, and only the Sea Witch could help her.

 Stir the blue coloring into the lemonade.

"I'll make you human," said the Sea Witch, "but you must give me something in return." So the mermaid gave her all that she had left to give—the last of her seven magical tears. Drop by drop, she added her blue treasures to the witch's cauldron.

 Add six more drops of blue coloring to the bowl and stir.

Once she drank the witch's potion, the little mermaid instantly found herself near the home of the sailor where three small islands floated above the blue sea. She now had legs instead of a mermaid's tail, but the witch had taken her voice. When she found the sailor, she could only tell her story through dancing. And oh how she danced! All three islands seemed to whirl with the amazing way she moved her new feet.

Add three scoops of pineapple sherbet (or sorbet) to the bowl and stir around in the lemonade until they have nearly melted.

But the sailor didn't understand the mermaid's story or remember that she rescued him from the storm. So in despair, the mermaid returned to the sea and swam out as far as she could. But without her mermaid's tail, she started to sink beneath the bubbling waves.

 Add the soda to the bowl and gently stir.

But the ocean was always kind to the little mermaid, and in a last act of pity, it turned her into the white foam that bubbles on top of the sea. And some say, if you listen carefully, you can still hear her story when the sea foam rolls in on the gentle waves.

 Ladle the lemonade into cups and listen for the mermaid's voice.

THE FIZZY FROG PRINCE

SPARKLING GREEN-SLIME PUNCH

Makes Six Cups

THIS STORY NEEDS:

1 cup (250 ml) water
1 cup (250 ml) orange juice
1 box (3 ounces / 85 g) melon or lime gelatin
(or plain with 2 drops of green food dye)
Ginger ale (about 6 cups / 1.5 L)

There once was a beautiful princess who lived near a deep, dark forest. In the middle of the forest was a little pond where the princess liked to sit on hot summer days. If she ever got bored, she would take out her golden ball, throw it up in the air, and catch it. But one day, the golden ball slipped from her fingers and fell into the little pond.

Pour the water into a small pot. Add the orange juice.

The princess tried to reach for the ball, but the pond was too deep. Just as she began to cry, tiny bubbles suddenly appeared on the surface of the water.

Place the pot on the stove over high heat until the water begins to boil.

The bubbles belonged to a slimy green frog who stuck his slimy green head out of the water. "Is this yours?" he asked the princess. He opened his mouth and out plopped the golden ball.

Turn off the heat, add the gelatin to the pot, and stir until completely dissolved.

"You may thank me with a kiss," said the frog, puckering his lips towards the princess. "Yuck!" she yelled, and ran off with the ball back to her castle, forgetting all about the frog and the kindness he had shown her. The next day, the frog hopped his way to the princess' castle and said, "You forgot my kiss, dear little miss." The princess had no intention of kissing a slimy frog, so she locked him away in the castle's coldest, darkest dungeon so that he wouldn't bother her anymore.

 Ladle the mixture into a baking dish and put into the freezer for one hour.

Locked in the cold dungeon, the frog loudly cried and croaked—the princess couldn't bear the noise any longer. She opened the dungeon door and found the poor little creature nearly frozen on the floor.

When the mixture is partially frozen, but still slushy enough to scoop, remove the baking dish from the freezer.

Feeling sorry for what she had done, the princess scooped the frog into her hand, slimy and cold as he was, and gave him the warmest kiss she could give.

With a large spoon or ice cream scooper, put one scoop of the green slush into individual cups.

There was magic in that kiss, for bright and fizzy bubbles surrounded the frog and turned him round and round until he finally turned into a handsome prince. And so goes the lesson of this tale—with a little love, something green and slimy might just turn into something very special.

Pour a cup of ginger ale over each scoop of green slush and stir it up for a slimy treat.

THE UGLY CHOCLING

WHITE SWANS HOT CHOCOLATE

Serves Two

THIS STORY NEEDS:

1 cup (250 ml) milk
1 cup (250 ml) half-and-half (single cream)
½ cup (100 g) butterscotch morsels
Mini marshmallows
¼ teaspoon vanilla extract
1 tablespoon cocoa powder

Long ago, in a lovely corner of the country, there flowed a river as white as cream. While the other animals were playing in the river, a mother duck sat patiently on her nest, keeping her eggs warm and cozy.

 Pour the milk and half-and-half (cream) into a small pot. Place the pot on the stove over medium heat.

When her nest got warm enough to steam, the eggs began to crack open. One by one, the little ducklings emerged from the nest and waddled down to the river for their first swim.

 When the milk begins to steam (before it boils), turn the heat down to low, add the butterscotch morsels, and whisk until they have melted into the milk.

But one of these ducklings looked very different from the rest. Pudgy and white, he was nothing like his brothers and sisters with their fluffy brown feathers. "My, what an ugly duckling!" said the other animals along the riverbank. They tried to fix the little creature by sprinkling him with perfume and washing off his ugliness in the river.

 Add one marshmallow to the pot along with the vanilla extract and whisk.

Scrubbing him didn't seem to work, so they tried to hide his ugliness by covering him all over in powdery dirt. But the dirt soon washed off, and the ugly duckling felt as if nothing could fix him. Crying big sad tears, he swam far down the river, away from the other animals, where a waterfall poured into a small round pool.

 Add the cocoa powder to the pot and whisk until combined in the milk. Using a ladle, pour the hot chocolate into mugs.

"Why are you crying?" said a kind voice nearby. The duckling looked up to see a family of birds floating across the pool. They were all large and white, just like him. And under their gentle wings he realized he wasn't an ugly duckling at all. He was a swan, the most beautiful bird of all!

 Add some marshmallows to each mug and watch as the white swans swim in their chocolaty pool!